Ghost Dance

by Aimee Nicole

Curious Corvid Publishing, LLC

Cover Art by Ravven White
Licensed through Shutterstock

ISBN: 978-1-959860-28-0

Printed in the United States of America

Curious Corvid Publishing, LLC

PO Box 204

Geneva, OH 44041

www.curiouscorvidpublishing.com

First Edition

Curious Corvid
PUBLISHING

For Ravven–

Who has always believed in my dreams and
welcomed me into her story with widespread wings.

10% of all proceeds from this collection will be donated to The Trevor Project by the author.

Our community is so diverse, rich in history, and worthy of love. We all deserve to thrive.

— Aimee Nicole

'Cause karma is the thunder

Rattling your ground

Karma's on your scent like a bounty hunter

Karma's gonna track you down

Step by step from town to town

Sweet like justice

Karma is a queen

—Taylor Swift

Gwisin: The ghost of a once living person (often a woman) found in Korean folklore. Oftentimes portrayed as a faceless, transparent being with long black hair. Gwisin often stay tied to the living realm to seek their revenge before crossing over...

Table of Contents

Swipe left

    left

    left

    left...

so many fish

pecking lips

phony Phils philosophising.

Send me more than just

a body.

I need something to hold onto

with both hands

      bleating heart

      bleached hair,

while I circle the clogged drain

mourning my time here until

POP

release,

and onto the next...

Looking for (Him)

friends

dates

casual hangs

possibly something serious

> Looking for (Me)
>
> friends
>
> something serious
>
> (enchant me
>
> entrance me
>
> don't ever let me
>
> go...)

Dressers emptied onto the bed.

Every single item a mismatch

and I wonder how I have ever

left this apartment looking

like a put together human.

Back to blank canvas—

jump into the shower

to calm these nerves.

Rub on some coconut body butter.

Apply shiny lip gloss,

I'm 15 again.

Finally ready to pull myself together,

he's lucky to have booked this date with me.

A Gemini with more bite

than a great white.

More love to give than

a Hallmark greeting card store.

I slip on shoes and grab my keys

hanging by the door,

twist the lock shut and depart.

Journey three blocks south under the full moon.

$10 cash

 a barter in 2025—

 violet stamp to inner wrist.

Old enough to drink/

 old enough to dream.

Part beautiful bodies to the bar

Bourbon neat laid to rest

 and I wait.

And I wished most to dance that night away...

stars gleaming so bright

we couldn't be captured on film.

Maybe finally the constellations would align

for my truest love to chart their path home.

I'd been waiting here all these years to build a house

from stones.

The only difference between

his $85 scotch and my $13 bourbon

is the hangover and a wallet filled with

dreams.

Excuse myself~

weave between bodies tinned on the dance
floor.

Bodies slick with sweat and tall tales and
unwavering hope.

Lock myself into the only empty stall,

take a deep, full-lunged breath.

Text my sister: *I'm taking him home.*

Response: *Be safe. Text me when he leaves!*

Emerge to tease my hair out in the mirror,

pinch both cheeks

step out into the unknown.

Keys clatter against metal

apartment door

swings wide

opens entry

to fate.

Drape coats across kitchen countertop,

shroud mail waiting to be sorted.

He steals a glance towards the fridge.

Thirsty? I ask.

Make yourself at home, I'll get us some drinks.

Words I'd come to regret.

A home

I'd come to wish

I had never shared.

I press a palm

to our team photo

magneted to fridge

in glossy glory.

Pre-game ritual,

tomorrow the season opener.

Their glassy eyes grinning back,

White Claws tipped toward the sun.

Our last game in pink Pride jerseys

(retired after Brad's passing last June).

A silent prayer for all that we lost,

a family built upon scars carved into bone.

Was it the way he came,

more violent than lightning

striking your path,

singeing its memory into

every moment (past and present).

Was it the way I came gently

like rain stroking

flower petals,

a fingertip trailing

across lips at midnight...

so gentle you cannot

be sure if it was dream

or reality.

No, I never saw it coming,

but I felt every fist land

and every tooth break free

from gum.

When the knife entered spleen

I sighed relief...

it would all end soon.

Please just leave me

alone to reminisce.

So many loved ones to recall.

So many mistakes to forgive.

Why did I have to wear

that slutty mesh top on a first date they are going to

think I'm a damn paid escort—no shade/no shame—

but damnit I can't even defend myself it's his word

against mine which is raindrops quickly being

swallowed by the ocean.

And I am there

like a beached whale so out of place offending all the
children who want to play

in the sand.

Family, friends, previous lovers cannot turn away in
their frames they are paralyzed in this

moment with me.

Like a magician he is dusting scrubbing disappearing
all the ways to trap him and I cannot alert a

single breathing soul.

He's pretending to be me, cleans up our glassware
and loads the dishwasher, wiping the

doorknob when he parts.

Only one clue remains, a single fingerprint on the
start button of the dishwasher, not even his

shifty shadow left behind.

And my spirit won't depart from this body,

pried with such screaming force.

I don't know them,

I can't leave me.

No one to speak,

no one to listen.

Urgent eviction

without appeal.

God's plan/

I cannot dispute the terms of my lease.

Rip every fingernail from the bed on the way out

on injustice sharp as a scythe.

Sun pulls itself

—heavy lidded—

peaks over horizon.

Raises the alarm,

a rising day

full of new promise.

15 unread text messages.

10 missed phone calls.

8:23AM the sun rises.

8:42AM the police are let into

my apartment by the landlord.

Photos taken in the worst lighting,

flash flashing flashily against my bruises

so I become less of a person

more of the murdered.

Collect my   phone

               keys

               wallet

               clothing littered across the floor like
fast food wrappers.

Dust the   door

               table

               bed (which we never made it to).

No one notices the dishwasher.

Ghost Dance - Aimee Nicole

Our mazes vary greatly,

and still we claw forward

leaving torn and bloodied

fingernails along the track.

Cover up with cover ups,

convince ourselves trauma

is just another beauty mark.

This body was made to be

read but never listen.

The days trickle by like an

icicle melting to memory.

My hearing turns the

dial slowly down to static.

Please speak up I'm not ignoring you.

Please speak up, did you hear my order correctly?

Please, no, I never ordered any of this at all.

I won't ghost dance

to raise spirits from their graves.

No, I'm pounding soundless

soles on your cracked laminate floor

calling you across the veil.

This is a ghost dance filled with poison apples

just one taste for you to buckle,

kneel for me.

Leave all your worldly possessions,

they have no value here.

Leave your friends behind,

they cannot enter.

Join me and pay for your crimes—

eternity awaits.

It's so cold here,

blueberry lips

tough as marble.

I'm running

out of places

to hide from

the grim reapers.

They never tire

of tracking my movement.

Hide in the tiniest

of dressers and teeniest

of drawers awaiting my arrival.

Patience has turned from

weakness to greatest soldier.

Maybe one day,

I would make

a good grim reaper.

Evaders cannot all

be seeking revenge,

some must be avoiding

their judgment.

And no one is better to deliver.

Perched from above,

crouching down below...

I track his moves   stealthily

                  steadily

                  surefooted.

A scientist observing

the rat.

Prepared in its cage

for slaughter.

April 11th

Tuesday

6:00AM — Most annoying alarm of all time

6:01AM — Morning shit

6:10AM — Disgusting protein shake thing

6:30AM — Gym

7:30AM — Shower, dress for work, news playing in background

8:30AM-4:30PM — Work, one hour lunch break (steak and four eggs)

5:00PM — Visit with mom in the nursing home, they play backgammon (she wins) then eat

dinner together in the dining room with her roommate Cheryl (who collects forgotten love letters)

7:00PM — Lays in bed and swipes on apps, chats, attempts to set up a date for Friday evening

10:00PM — Lights out, unfortunately not forever

I've always been like a snake,

so quick to shed my home

again and again.

Keep the load light and feathery,

able to wisp away when called.

Now that my body

can no longer house tomorrow,

all I want is to

keep the weight on

and carry it forward.

I discovered my secret

the following Monday

during a rainstorm.

Tracking him through

a department store

while he picked out a

grotesque beige tie

for a company party.

Leaned over his shoulder

with eyes rolling

toward the heavens

and saw my own reflection

staring back.

Nose a bit concave and

lips smudged to memory,

but there was no mistaking me.

He tightened the knot,

looked up to meet my gaze,

and let out a shriek so loud

even the grim reapers came running.

I most miss dreaming.

Every night vicious

horrors flick across closed lids/

a picture I cannot escape from.

I can no longer blink...

eyes permanent projectors

of the terrors I must bear witness to

and document in blood.

His fingers paint the keys

with my blood,

wicked wishes chanted upon

a waxing moon.

Baited traps lain so sweetly,

their lips will never

taste poison until

fingers clench the heart

ready to squeeze.

Ghost Dance - Aimee Nicole

Sunday funday-

breakfast always ready,

waiting with the mobile orders.

The same sagging cold brew,

bacon, egg and cheese

slabbed on a plain bagel.

Maybe he will die of

clogged arteries before the trial,

save us all the trouble

of seeing his ugly mug

splashed across Page Six.

One day...

I just want some punk teenager

to snatch his frothy coffee,

make him pay twice

and wait in line like the rest of us.

The

long plastic

bag rustles in my closet,

protects the carefully tailored

outfit I'll never wear to my sister's wedding.

Someone

needs to turn

off that desk fan

before it overheats,

starts a fire that spreads

from floor to floor. The smoking

gun to warn us that vengeance is coming.

Emails ping into her inbox,

stack like leftovers.

Forget, forgetting, forgotten.

She stares out the window at

nothing and everything.

A pigeon balancing upon a live wire.

The french fry food truck

slowly working through the lunch rush.

A meter maid chalking tires

once an hour on the hour.

The world continues

to tick by slowly...

quicksand that swallows you

slowly then all at once.

I bang so hard on the glass.

Everyone keeps hacking at their

pot roast and stabbing their carrots

like there wasn't just a murder in the family.

Peas spill onto the floor unnoticed,

crushed into the aubergine rug

beneath discount outlet soles.

I'm here, outside, watching you slice

across the "27" iced atop the

grocery store sheet cake.

Your cheeks even more sallow,

pallid in the flickering candlelight.

We are both questioning how tasteless

it is to number this celebration when

I am a corpse not yet decomposed.

Happy birthday to you.

I'm watching him lift those

stupid weights at the gym

on a Tuesday when the police

arrive unannounced.

A warrant issued for his arrest.

Everyone stops   lifting

cycling

jogging...

waits for his reaction.

No, he can't go to the

station right now,

he has a deadline and

needs to head to the office.

You can call them from the precinct.

He doesn't phone the office,

uses his one call

on his pledge

brother from college—

now a practicing attorney

at some big shot law firm

in the city.

Threaded together with

fraternity secrets, a duty to

protect runs thicker than blood.

Tomorrow he will have

the initial arraignment.

Must be able to speak

clearly through his teeth

not guilty

and be believed...

The courthouse is

bigger than I remember.

A theatre featuring many

plays running in synchrony.

Costume: Business casual.

Set: Grunge, aging, mixed media.

Sound: Desperate.

Lighting: Dim.

Performer: Murderer, guilty.

Audience: Ready to gasp on cue.

Fit to stand trial

Trial by jury

Court date set: October 21st

9:00AM

Request for a closed court: Denied.

Released on bond.

I don't notice the weeks

slip past, I'm too busy

watching

waiting

wishing

everyone is competent enough

to present my presence

because I'm just a memory

that haunts and hunts

for a better tomorrow.

When the day finally arrives,

I ride in the car with my sister.

Spent so much time with

the monster, I'd neglected her.

We ascend the steps in tandem,

go through security,

pause outside the court door.

Are we ready to face what awaits inside?

We have no choice but to enter.

Ghost Dance - Aimee Nicole

It's a sensational sensation.

Reporters sit in the back,

a court packed with curiosity.

Who will be held accountable

for this crime?

Will it be the man who

wielded his fists to

smother out of a life?

Angle: Gay just looking for a fun

night out killed in shocking murder

shakes town, who is safe?

Or will it be society/media/entertainment/

parents/community/first amendment rights?

Angle: The media is poisoning

our children and making them violent!!!

My state flag flutters

behind the judge's bench.

A homeland where I buried

my dreams

(and my lies).

I wonder, today,

will she bleed for me,

or leave me to

starve on broken promises.

He walks into the court-

starched plaid button down

suggested by the lawyer.

Looks like a picnic table,

    ready for me to lay

    my spread across his back.

    Make quite the mess.

    Grind butter knives

    down to stubs.

    Pick up my napkin

    to wipe that smirk sideways.

    Everything left is for the birds

    until all that remains is bone.

Right hand on the Bible

meaningless mutterings

promises promises

on worthless relics

thin as air papers that flutter in a spring
breeze

swears to a God

not present

Pleads not guilty,

alibi loose as cremated ash.

I'm innocent Your Honor!

Reading poetry at home

stroking my adopted cat.

She needs diabetes medication

every 4 hours.

I'm the sole caretaker.

Responsible.

Trustworthy.

A valued,

hardworking

American Citizen.

Prosecutor presents

(lack of) evidence

Could not be bothered to

dust the dishwasher...

too busy sipping their

flat whites and talking about

changes to company PTO

that just came out over the weekend.

Photos of my body

displayed on a screen

big enough to show those

blackheads I'd tried

to treat for weeks.

Gasps from the audience

like this is a reality show

and I'd gotten botched

plastic surgery.

But no, I was alive and breathing

until suddenly there was

no breath left in me—

only the thirst for revenge.

Prosecutor calls Mrs. Kleine to the stand.

Defense objects with a shout!

We don't have her on the list!

We are not prepared!

Judge demands both counselors approach the bench.

Prosecutor explains that Mrs. Kleine was

held as a secret witness to protect

her privacy and safety.

Defense schoolgirl giggles and mocks.

Judge pulls down his very large readers

and glares at the defense:

Overruled.

Mrs. Kleine sits down neatly,

clutching her purse through

pristine white gloved hands.

She surveys the court to see who came

out to support her testimony today.

Turns out, no additional bodies pack in,

as she was a surprise witness.

She gives a small wave to the

cameras at the back of the court.

Her black skirt is perfectly starched

and white lace socks peekaboo from

her Mary Janes.

Her testimony begins.

Mrs. Kleine was awake

watching her late night murder mysteries and knitting hats for the local children's hospital that night. She heard banging from my apartment, a rare occurrence, especially for that time of night. I was a very quiet and respectful neighbor. She set down her knitting supplies and went to watch out the peephole, stepping up on the stool set by the door for such occasions. You can go check, it's still there. She always keeps it ready in case she needs to check on the neighbors. See, sometimes there are strangers that lurk in the hall. She always reports them to the landlord. There are call records, you can check those too. Anyway, after exactly 57 minutes according to her Anne Klein watch (which she bought because they almost have the same exact name), a man left the apartment across the hall with red smeared across his cheek. Red splattered his shirt by the shoulder too. She saw it there.

Of course she can point him out in the courtroom, he's sitting right there at the defense table. Didn't try to cover up with a hat or anything. That bastard just thought he could walk right out of the building without any of us noticing anything!

.

So many years I fed Mrs. Kleine's

cats while she visited her sister in Colorado,

and I never realized she kept such a close eye on me.

Didn't know how important these small

connections we make in life can be.

How monumental the significance of

a nosy neighbor who insists you take

stale butter cookies home

every Sunday because you

look a little too skinny.

Jury on recess.

I sit next to my sister

on the toilets while she

stares at the graffitied stall.

Sarah <3's Tony

Never Give Up.

Men always cheat.

I don't know what I would write.

Did I live long enough to

earn wisdom like a degree?

There were so many things

I still wanted to   explore

                                                 see

                                                 feel.

I always wanted to see the

Rocky Mountains,

ascend higher towards the heavens

until I wasn't sure if I was still

amongst the living or the damned.

She's getting angry,

second guessing the

community college

degree prosecutor.

Which seems aggressive

and I side eye her since

I Know She Knows

my community college

degree afforded me

a clean break from

the home that could not

hold me.

Slams her fist against the sink now,

scares a woman out from the

toilet without washing her hands.

Wondering if second degree murder

is a wish upon a shooting star

on a cloudy night.

Maybe voluntary homicide

would have fit the justice system.

Not the crime,

but the cage we fit into.

Judge: Foreman, has the jury reached a verdict?

Foreman: Yes, your Honor.

On count one,

the charge of a hate crime,

we find the defendant:

Not guilty.

On count two,

the charge of second degree murder,

we find the defendant:

not guilty.

Judge: Thank you for your time and verdict.

Mr. Salter, you are free to go.

Split like a broken heart

no bridge wide enough to reach

decisions wielded in permanent ink...

unity a dream forgotten on playgrounds.

She picks up her coat,

swings it around her shoulders,

walks from the courtroom without

even the click clack of footsteps—

a body that refuses to break silence.

Refuses to look at the man

who murdered her sibling.

There is nothing to say,

only vast oceans of forgiveness

to conjure from a desert.

But I watch him take this

verdict like a thief,

tuck it safely in his wallet

as PROOF he is INNOCENT.

So ready to whip it out

like a store membership,

flash it to anyone who

is ready to receive.

But no, it's never so simple

to clear one's name.

Even a whiteboard will

leave the trace of marker behind.

Write over the memory of lesson

again and again.

Hope for a better outcome

if only you have learned

from past mistakes.

And he is furious.

All those carefully crafted dating profiles

reported

reviewed

removed.

Still...you can never fully erase a criminal

from the underbelly of the Internet.

Only takes one cold winter night for him

to replace them

with stranger's photos,

ready to release himself on the

dating pool all over again.

One ping and he matches with another,

little does he know he's the bait.

Unsuspecting

and unprepared for what awaits him

at the same bar we met

just six months ago.

Nate shows up in a loose fitting Hawaiian

shirt to hide all his muscle mass,

built to compete in professional circuits.

I look on amused, anticipating.

Nate recognizes him right away,

sees through the catfish excuses,

reads the paper every morning with

his protein shake before training.

A plan is hatched...

and deliver us from evil...

Nate rolls his eyes at the

expensive liquor.

Holds onto patience like

an heirloom,

so precious, must protect it

with all his might.

Declines the cab and lures Mr. Murder

to the river with the promise

of discretion, privacy, and

yes they can pick up a bottle of

Macallan on the way.

The bottomless river where

so many electric scooters disappear

in drunken pranks.

The bottomless river that

leads out to the bay.

The bottomless river where crimes

are forgotten in just one swallow.

⁂

Gay hate crimes are

stones thrown

into fires already burning wild.

No, they can never tame us.

Freer than the weeds

overtaking perfectly manicured lawns.

A golf course strewn with

signs screaming "Members Only,"

yet we show up after hours drunk

on cheap Narragansetts

and fuck on the 9th hole—

leave our bodies pressed so

hard into the turf they need

to sow from seed all over again.

I surrender

myself.

Two very exhausted

grim reapers

ready to take me

under.

Accept their

Very Important Proposal.

Not ready to be reborn

as a politician's wife

or doting King

or dog with grooming appointments

every other Tuesday

and a personal masseuse

and food made by

the live-in chef.

Rather track down the most vile,

extract them from most secret depressions,

drag them out by the throat

to make them face confession.

Ghost Dance - Aimee Nicole

Aimee Nicole is a chronically ill/disabled, queer poet currently residing in Rhode Island. She holds a B.F.A. in Creative Writing from Roger Williams University and has been published by various lit mags. Her poetry collections include *Daily Worship* (Laughing Ronin Press), *Panoramic* (Curious Corvid Publishing), *Consequences of 50 Shades* (A Thin Slice of Anxiety Press), and *Master of the Universe* (Back Room Poetry). She also has a choose your own adventure titled *My Kink Adventure* (Curious Corvid Publishing). Feel free to direct message or tag her in any K-drama recommendations on her Instagram @aimeenicole525.